I0762331

GRANDMA,
I made you a
BOOK

DEAR GRANDMA,

I made this book for you because you're an amazing grandma.

Thank you for all that you do and all the ways you help me grow. I've included some of them here in these pages, but there are just too many to fit into one book.

I made this especially for you because you really are one of a kind.

Love,

HERE'S ME!

I have lots of happy memories with you!

Here's a picture of us

when we ______________

so we can always remember.

SPENDING TIME WITH YOU
IS EXTRA SPECIAL.

I ESPECIALLY LIKE

____

____

WITH YOU.

Since you're one of
my favorite people,

I used my favorite color to draw these flowers for you.

You are one of the greatest people ever. You might be better than...

(check the boxes)

☐ Playing on a tropical island beach

☐

(WRITE YOUR OWN!)

I like to tell people about my grandma.

Here's a list of words I use to describe you:

WE LOVE EACH OTHER SO MUCH! HERE, I DREW TWO HEARTS FOR US:

When I think of you, I feel...

(check the boxes)

☐

(WRITE YOUR OWN!)

So, here's a
BIG THANK-YOU
HIGH FIVE
for being so awesome.

(Trace hand)

You deserve a GAZILLION MORE!

I KNOW YOU
CARE ABOUT ME
A LOT WHEN
YOU...

Together or apart, we're always sending love to each other.

Look! I drew a package of

____

just for you.

You're exactly the perfect grandma for me because...

HERE,
LET ME
GIVE YOU
THIS
AWARD.

WORLD'S
GRANDMA

Sometime, let's

together. Wouldn't that be so fun?

Thank you, Grandma.
Because of you, I know that...
(check the boxes)

☐ You are always there for me

☐ We'll have lots more ADVENTURES

☐ I AM LOVED

☐ You help me be ME

☐

(WRITE YOUR OWN!)

BECAUSE
OF YOU,
WE ARE A
FAMILY.

Written by: Miriam Hathaway
Illustrated by: Asahi Nagata
Edited by: Bailey Vega
Art Directed by: Justine Edge

An imprint of the Crown Publishing Group
A division of Penguin Random House LLC
1745 Broadway, New York, NY 10019
live-inspired.com | penguinrandomhouse.com

ISBN: 978-1-957891-70-5 | CPSIA: A012509001

1st printing. Manufactured in China with soy inks on FSC®-Mix certified paper.

The authorized representative in the EU for product safety and compliance is Penguin Random House Ireland, Morrison Chambers, 32 Nassau Street, Dublin D02 YH68, Ireland, https://eu-contact.penguin.ie.

Create meaningful moments with gifts that inspire.

CONNECT WITH US
live-inspired.com | sayhello@compendiuminc.com

@compendiumliveinspired
#compendiumliveinspired